When Ann came out, she
had a box.
Grace tried to take a look.

"What is it? What is it?
What could it be?
Would you open it up?
Let me look and see!"

What Could It Be?

by Judy Nayer
illustrated by Bob Berry

Scott Foresman

Editorial Offices: Glenview, Illinois • New York, New York
Sales Offices: Reading, Massachusetts • Duluth, Georgia
Glenview, Illinois • Carrollton, Texas • Menlo Park, California

Ann took longer than she
should have.
Grace stood and tapped her foot.

"Oh, no! Don't look!
You must try to guess.
You should ask me some things.
I'll say no or yes."

"Is it bigger than a fly?
Is it smaller than a book?
Is it something made of wood?
Is it something great to cook?"

"It's bigger than a fly.
It's even larger than a book.
It's much softer than wood.
It would not be good to cook!"

"If I shook it, would it break?
Is it beautiful to see?
Can we play with it together?
Would you please show me?"

"The answers you are looking
for are no, yes, and yes!
Should I show you?
No, I shouldn't.
I still want you to guess!"

"It's not the biggest
or the smallest thing.
That much I should know.
We could play with it together.
Is it a great big ball to throw?"

"It could be, but it isn't.
It is not something to throw.
It's now no longer than a foot.
But it's something that will grow!"

"It's something that can grow?
Oh, that is good to know!
If it can grow, it could become
the largest thing I know!"

"I know what you are thinking.
But it just could not be.
So come a little closer
and you will see . . .

the most beautiful, cuddliest,
softest, and furriest, greatest
new friend for you and me!"

"Meet my beautiful new puppy!"